BECOMING

Charleston, SC
www.PalmettoPublishing.com

Becoming
Copyright © 2023 by Shakayla Dickey

All rights reserved
No portion of this book may be reproduced, stored in a retrieval system, or transmitted in any form by any means–electronic, mechanical, photocopy, recording, or other–except for brief quotations in printed reviews, without prior permission of the author.

First Edition

Paperback ISBN: 979-8-8229-2850-3

BECOMING

SHAKAYLA DICKEY

CONTENTS

Chapter 1: Love 1

Chapter 2: Me.................................... 2

Chapter 3: Love?................................. 3

Chapter 4: Dream Dad 4

Chapter 5: New Beginning 5

Chapter 6: Why?................................. 6

Chapter 7: Uncovered Truths..................... 7

Chapter 8: New Love 8

Chapter 9: Peace................................. 9

Chapter 10: Realizations.......................... 10

Chapter 11: Emotions 11

Chapter 12: Potential............................. 12

Chapter 13: Mom 13

Chapter 14: Twenty-Third Birthday 14

Chapter 15: I Don't Want to Be Foolish... 15

Chapter 16: Men.................................. 16

Chapter 17: Sip................................... 17

Chapter 18: Him.................................. 19

Chapter 19: I Love You 20

Chapter 20: Journey.............................. 21

DEDICATIONS:

To whom this book was inspired by and originally written for. God and my childhood self. Thank you, God, for pushing and placing this work of art onto me, giving me an outlet during a transformative moment and time in my life and persistent guidance. For you only know my heart and love to/from its deepest core. Thank you, child Shakayla. It fills my heart with love and joy knowing that I'm making us proud. Achieving one of our dreams of writing and publishing our first book. I vividly remember that day of us in the library and telling ourselves we're going to publish a book someday. We didn't know when, where, what, or how. Just that we'd know when it was time. That day came. We said we'd do it and we did. About 14 or 15 years later, but we did it! May we continue shining our light, love and chasing our dreams.

Chapter 1

Love

NOVEMBER 30, 2020, 7:58 P.M.

"Love is patient, love is kind. It does not envy or boast. It is not arrogant or rude. It does not insist on its way; it is not irritable or resentful. It does not rejoice at wrongdoing but rejoices with the truth."

1 Corinthians 13:4-8a

Chapter 2

Me

NOVEMBER 30, 2020, 8:03 P.M.

I asked myself who I would be without the influences, opinions, and mannerisms of others. I see glimpses of my true self, and it's gotten better over time. I'm learning to get out of my head, and it has improved. Slowly but surely, as I age and become a woman, I find and love myself more and more every day.

Chapter 3

Love?

DECEMBER 8, 2020

Have you ever missed the feeling of love? Have you longed for profound affection, tenderness, and intimacy? It's as if I've lost hope, which is seemingly unattainable. Wanting to be in a relationship shouldn't be unrealistic. I frequently question that. Am I withholding from you? Am I not taking the risks?

Chapter 4

Dream Dad

JANUARY 3, 2021, 8:26 P.M.

I dreamed of you, dreamed about the complexion of your skin, the shape of your body, and the appearance of your structure. The characteristics, personalities, and features that you may possess. As I awakened, I recalled a vivid childhood memory. I was sitting in a chair inside a classroom, surrounded by children and a teacher. A man walked through the door. He pulled his child into him with an embrace. Soon after, more fathers started to follow along, doing the same to their offspring. I looked around the room, noticing the joy, laughter, and happiness surrounding me. I turned my head to the door. Even though I knew that you wouldn't show up, there was a part of me silently hoping that you would.

Chapter 5
New Beginning

JANUARY 6, 2020, 2:58 P.M.

Did you ever sense that you were reaching your potential? Like everything you ever dreamed of was so close that you could feel it? Like you could taste, touch, see, and hear it? That's what this moment feels like. As if I'm on the verge of a defining moment in my life. Everything in life that I want, I can get. Maybe the only thing that's stopping me is me. Not anymore.

Chapter 6

Why?

JANUARY 15, 2021, 1:42 P.M.

Why ask for my number to only text it once? Why ask me on a date and never make official plans as to when and where? Why speak as if your intentions are pure? Why? I tried to hide my feelings and not like you as much as I do... did. But I couldn't. I wanted to be with you, next to you, but it didn't seem to be mutual. Those feelings came to a standstill when I realized they weren't being reciprocated. I liked how I felt. I just wish I had felt this way for the right man instead of the wrong one.

Chapter 7

Uncovered Truths

MARCH 29, 2021, 2:04 P.M.

I've learned so much about myself, especially when it comes to dating. I realized that I didn't know what I wanted or needed from a relationship. I wonder if I had been willing to be with someone who I thought would've been "great" for me, but now I know I wouldn't have been. I have no interest in anyone. I am content with the lessons learned from my bad dealings with men—lessons I do not wish to repeat. To those men, you hurt and broke me. I needed that. It led me to me.

Chapter 8

New Love

MAY 28, 2021, 5:21 P.M.

Through music, I've found love and a gentle, warm embrace. I feel my beauty, my heart, my love, and my spirit. I also see the scars, marks, and bruises. Losing and finding yourself isn't such a bad thing. It can create freedom and happiness, feelings I hope never go away. I found the sun in a dark haven.

Chapter 9

Peace

JUNE 17, 2021, 4:35 P.M.

Oftentimes, I lie on my bedroom floor and look up at the ceiling and around the room. Not a lot of thoughts come to my mind. I don't question that. I let it be. I know that when this happens, I'm at peace. Peace within myself and the world. I want to carry that feeling of peace everywhere I go.

Chapter 10

Realizations

AUGUST 2, 2021, 5:52 P.M.

I neglected and avoided my own feelings and emotions. It wasn't intentional—at least, not in the beginning—but over time, I started to get into a habit and stopped caring about them. I feel like I've been experiencing this for weeks, but it could have been longer. That's over now. I'm ready to make another change. More positivity, more love, and more peace.

Chapter 11

Emotions

AUGUST 15, 2021, 5:03 P.M.

The emotions that I felt were hidden, closeted, and closed have reopened. It hurts to try to reconnect with those feelings again, but they're back. They are my strongest assets. I feel to feel, create, and be.

Chapter 12

Potential

AUGUST 26, 2021, 5:49 P.M.

I didn't expect to like or be with you. Nor enjoy deep conversations and listen to your voice as you express yourself. It's unbelievable that I've fallen for you in four days. I expect the disappointment or fall-off, yet you've shown yourself to be different. The closest things that I can relate this feeling to are in books and movies. The kind of happiness and joy I get from you daily.

Chapter 13

Mom

AUGUST 28, 2021, 10:26 P.M.

It was frightening watching you fall ill and suffer. This was the first time we'd seen you like this. For the first time in a long time, I wondered what it would be like to lose you. It is an unthinkable idea to contemplate. I tried to stay away from it, to divert the thought. I'm not ready for the loss of my mother. We've got a long journey ahead of us. We survived it all, and we'll do the same now. We'll get through it. I love you with all my heart.

Chapter 14

Twenty-Third Birthday

SEPTEMBER 11, 2021, 1:30 P.M.

I don't even know how to express myself. I'm twenty-three. It would probably be nice to hear an inspirational speech about being in your early twenties and not putting too much pressure on yourself and everything. Just to keep me from getting overwhelmed. As I'm lying down on the floor, writing this with a light from my phone shining on my journal, I realized it. I'm OK. All I want today—or on any other birthday—is to feel loved and appreciated. Hearing and reading the "Happy Birthday" messages and sweet words being recited by my loved ones, I am reminded of how grateful I am to those individuals who are still here. That's what matters in the end.

Chapter 15

I Don't Want to Be Foolish...

12:45 P.M.

I desire to be open and expressive but at the same time to remain vulnerable and protective. Ever since I've been with you, I've been this way. Struggling with both. Scared. Held back from the simplest, smallest things, like not reading or hearing your good-morning voice messages for three or four days to know if your feelings have changed. Hoping that you tell me.

Chapter 16

Men

SEPTEMBER 15, 2021, 1:14 P.M.

It's terrible, not knowing how valuable you are and wanting to be with someone so much that you believe that being disrespected and trampled on is acceptable. It's terrible, the way we allow men to treat us. Yearning for love and acceptance. After crying and grieving, you find yourself healing. Moving past it. It's when you're in a healthy relationship that you realize how those previous relationships affected you. Unwilling to give in, fearful of the outcome, second-guessing yourself, feeling too many emotions all at once and thinking about so much at the same time. I didn't want to tell you everything that was on my mind, but I want you to know everything.

Chapter 17

Sip

NOVEMBER 14, 2021, 2:46 P.M.

As I've grown up, I've learned a lot from your successes and failures. Your traumas, actions, and words. I'm aware of how and why you've done the things you've done and said the things you've said. You've been hurt. Conscious and subconsciously, you've suppressed and released that pain onto your children. Caused by your mother and passed down from her to you. I wish that you acknowledged and held yourself accountable for your actions. Drinking may be one of your greatest weaknesses and downfalls. It brings out the worst in you. You're stubborn. You can hold certain things over people's heads. Despite all of that and more, I know that you're hurt and in pain. You have a terrible way of addressing that. You have toxic traits. A good heart that can be overruled by the bad with one sip. I have faith that you can overcome it.

Chapter 18

Him

DECEMBER 4, 2021, 5:29 P.M.

The incredible being that you are, who listens, cares, supports, and is honest. It feels like searching for a needle in a haystack when I think of how there aren't many like you. The feelings that come from inside and are displayed on the outside come from the bliss that I have for you. I'm genuinely happy with you. I feel safe and welcome to fall in love with you. I may be guarded, but with you, I don't feel as though I have to keep that shield up. I feel the desire to expand my vocabulary, to find those words that perfectly resonate with my feelings. I find myself with these sentiments that I hope to have the grace to express to you one day.

Chapter 19

I Love You

DECEMBER 7, 2021, 2:33 P.M.

Last night was the first time we told each other, "I love you." Although I only had a partial sleep, I was deeply touched by the feelings I felt when I heard you say those words. You've told me you love me a lot. I love you too. I love you so much.

Chapter 20

Journey

DECEMBER 7, 2021

I've learned that life is a journey. There are many lessons to be learned, challenges to overcome, and lessons to be taught. Life is the greatest teacher you can have. Sometimes you are uncertain of the correct route. You're looking at your peers, comparing lives. A wonderful lesson I have learned thus far is to believe in yourself. Knowing better for yourself, your judgment, and the decisions of your life, you'll find your path.

AUTHOR'S BIOGRAPHY

I was born in Decatur, Illinois. The daughter of a single mother and middle child of two sisters. I reside in Texas where I also attend college as an Associates of Arts major. I am an author, actress and screenwriter. I enjoy reading, writing and spending time with my love ones. My contact information is my email Shakayladickey@icloud.com and my website is linktr.ee/Shakayladickey.

ACKNOWLEDGEMENTS:

To my mother, Michelle Dickey-Walker. Thank you for believing in me no matter what. You always believed in your children and their capabilities despite what us or others might've thought. You are a resilient woman with a beautiful heart and soul. Very caring, loving, selfless and silly. You have your children's back like on other. I couldn't be more thankful and grateful to God for creating you and making you, our mother. A phenomenal woman you are.

To youngest sister, Shakierra. You are the best youngest sibling one could ever ask for. I was fortunate for us to be close in age, grow up and be kids together. Our childhoods are intertwined. We've experienced the highs and lows, good and bad. Keeping each other afloat truly through the thick and thin. I love knowing that I got a partner in crime. You are an outstanding, strong and fierce young woman. I know you're going to take the world by storm and I'll be there in awe as you do. Keep your head up, always. JJ and Amari are blessed to have you as a mother and vice versa.

To Shakemia, my eldest sister. The bond that we share is unique one. I love you. I love our laughs, conversations, walks and funny moments. Despite being the oldest, you treated your younger siblings as your equals and we all stood strong as a unit together. You have a giving heart. Stay strong, truly know yourself, your worth and who you are. Sending love to your babies Kayden and Kayvon.

To the Palmetto Publishing team. Thank you to Josie and Stephanie for guiding me through this process, patience and honestly. Also, for helping make my dream come true.

Lastly, to all of my love ones that weren't mentioned, but are loved and appreciated nonetheless. None of it goes unnoticed. Thank you for everything.

www.ingramcontent.com/pod-product-compliance
Lightning Source LLC
LaVergne TN
LVHW092102060526
838201LV00047B/1529